Harper Lee

TO KILL A MOCKINGBIRD

EDITED AND ILLUSTRATED BY
Ruth Benton Blackmore

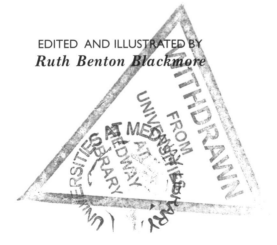

Hodder Murray
A MEMBER OF THE HODDER HEADLINE GROUP

Hachette's policy is to use papers that are natural, renewable and recyclable products and made from wood grown in sustainable forests. The logging and manufacturing processes are expected to conform to the environmental regulations of the country of origin.

Orders: please contact Bookpoint Ltd, 130 Milton Park, Abingdon, Oxon OX14 4SB. Telephone: (44) 01235 827720. Fax: (44) 01235 400454. Lines are open 9.00–5.00, Monday to Saturday, with a 24-hour message answering service. Visit our website at www.hoddereducation.co.uk

Copyright of original text from *To Kill A Mockingbird* © Harper Lee, 1960
© Ruth Benton Blackmore, 2007
Original series concept © Philip Page, 2006
First published in 2007 by
Hodder Murray, an imprint of Hodder Education,
an Hachette Livre UK company,
338 Euston Road
London NW1 3BH

Impression number	10 9 8 7 6 5 4 3 2 1
Year	2012 2011 2010 2009 2008 2007

Cover photo © Bill Fritsch/Brand X/Corbis
Typeset in Adobe Garamond 13pt by DC Graphic Design Limited, Swanley Village, Kent
Printed in Great Britain by Martins the Printers, Berwick Upon Tweed

A catalogue record for this title is available from the British Library

ISBN-13: 978 0340 940 105

Contents

Background

When *To Kill a Mockingbird* was first published in 1960, it was an instant success. It won the Pulitzer Prize for fiction in 1961 and was made into an award winning film in 1962.

Nelle Harper Lee was born in 1926 in Monroeville, Alabama, a small town in America's deep South. In 1929, the Great Economic Depression hit America. Every sector of society was affected, even the solid middle-class Lee family (her father was a lawyer) and there was great distress and hunger amongst the poor.

The southern states historically were agricultural and cotton-producing; cotton meant plantations and plantations meant slaves. Although the slaves were freed in 1865, racist attitudes remained and **segregation** was accepted as normal until the Civil Rights movement gained momentum in the late 1950s under the leadership of Martin Luther King.

segregation – the practice of separating the black communities from the white, e.g. in schools, on buses, in church and all public facilities

About the story

To Kill a Mockingbird is related by Scout (Jean Louise) Finch. The story begins in the early summer of 1933, when Scout is nearly six and ends at Halloween in the autumn of 1935. Scout lives in Maycomb, a small town in southern Alabama, and her father is a lawyer. Harper Lee used her own childhood experiences for the setting of her story.

The Finch family and Dill

Scout, her brother Jem, and their friend Dill*, play, argue, fight and learn together. They also encounter an adult world which is far from pleasant. They are watched over by Atticus, Jem and Scout's father, and when they meet ignorance, prejudice, racism and violence he is always there to explain and to guide.

Atticus

Atticus has a vision of a world that is fair, where all men are equal and capable of seeing another person's point of view – 'able to walk around in their shoes'. He believes in having the courage to stand up for what is right, however difficult or painful to do so.

The Mockingbird

The mockingbirds of the area do no harm – 'don't do one thing but sing their hearts out for us' – they are a symbol of all that is harmless and at the same time vulnerable and powerless. Atticus forbids Jem and Scout to shoot at mockingbirds with their air rifles. He says it would be a sin.

Sin

Maycomb is a seemingly happy, kindly society; but sin is at its very heart, as Scout and Jem are about to find out …

* Dill is said to be modelled on Harper Lee's childhood friend Truman Capote. He grew up to be a prolific writer and colourful character. His best-known films are *Breakfast at Tiffany's* and *In Cold Blood*.

Cast of characters

Uncle Jack Atticus's younger brother

Aunt Alexandra Older sister of Atticus, snobby and severe

Calpurnia Cook, housekeeper and mothers Jem and Scout

Atticus Finch Widower, lawyer and father of Scout and Jem

Jem Finch Thoughtful, long-suffering brother of Scout. He is nearly ten at the beginning of the story

Scout (Jean Louise) Finch Intelligent, curious, tomboy and fighter. She is nearly six at the beginning of the story

The Finch family and Calpurnia

Walter Cunningham Poor farmer

The Radley house Dark and spooky

Bob Ewell 'White trash'

Walter Cunningham Junior Schoolfriend of Scout and Jem

Heck Tate Sheriff

Tom Robinson Victim of racial prejudice

Miss Maudie Long-standing friend of the Finch family

Dill Lively friend of Scout and Jem

Friends, neighbours and an enemy

Part One

It is early summer 1933, Scout Finch is nearly six and her brother Jem is nearly ten. They are allowed to play within calling distance of Calpurnia, their housekeeper. The children's boundaries are Mrs Henry Lafayette Dubose's house to the north and the Radley house to the south, but they have their own boundaries. Mrs Dubose's house is to be avoided and the Radley place is too terrifying to go near.

Mrs H. L. Dubose

Miss Stephanie Crawford

Miss Maudie

Finch family

Miss Rachel (Dill's aunt)

To town

To school

The Radley house

Scout tells the story of the next two and a half years.

Maycomb was an old town, but it was a tired old town when I first knew it. In rainy weather the streets turned to red slop; grass grew on the sidewalks, the courthouse sagged in the square. Somehow, it was hotter then: a black dog suffered on a summer's day; bony mules hitched to **Hoover carts** flicked flies in the sweltering shade of the live oaks on the square. Men's stiff collars wilted by nine in the morning. Ladies bathed before noon, after their three-o'clock naps, and by nightfall were like soft teacakes with frostings of sweat and sweet talcum. We lived on the main residential street in town – Atticus, Jem and I, plus Calpurnia our cook.

Hoover carts – open carts drawn by horses or mules

 ● What does the description of wilting collars and frequent bathing tell you about the climate of Maycomb, Alabama?

Early one morning, Scout and Jem investigate a noise they hear next door in Miss Rachel Haverford's garden.

I'm Charles Baker Harris. I can read.

How old are you, four-and-a-half?

Goin' on seven.

Scout's been readin' ever since she was born. You look right puny.

I'm little but I'm old.

Why don't you come over?

Folks call me Dill.

Dill is from Meridian, a town 500 kilometres away. Lively and imaginative, his head is full of ideas, fancies and crazy plans. He is staying with his Aunt Rachel all summer and the children pass the weeks together. Dill is drawn to the Radley house, but none of them dare approach nearer than the lamp post a few metres away.

 ● What does Dill mean by 'I'm little but I'm old'?

2

Inside the house lived a **malevolent phantom**. People said he existed, but Jem and I had never seen him. People said he went out at night when the moon was down, and peeped in windows. When people's azaleas froze in a cold snap, it was because he had breathed on them. Any stealthy small crimes committed in Maycomb were his work. Once the town was terrorized by a series of **morbid nocturnal** events: people's chickens and household pets were found mutilated; although the culprit was Crazy Addie, who eventually drowned himself in Barker's Eddy, people still looked at the Radley Place, unwilling to discard their initial suspicions. A Negro would not pass the Radley Place at night, he would cut across to the sidewalk opposite and whistle as he walked. The Maycomb school grounds adjoined the back of the Radley lot; from the Radley chickenyard tall **pecan** trees shook their fruit into the schoolyard, but the **nuts** lay untouched by the children: Radley pecans would kill you. A baseball hit into the Radley yard was a lost ball and no questions asked.

malevolent phantom – evil ghost
morbid nocturnal – sickening night-time
pecan nuts – similar to walnuts

- Why do you think people preferred to suspect the occupant of the Radley house, rather than the person who actually injured the animals?
- Think about the difference between superstition and prejudice. Both imply a strongly-held belief not based on fact. Were the Radley pecan nuts really poisonous?

The 'malevolent phantom' is Arthur Radley – known as Boo. His father imprisoned him in the house when Boo got involved in some mild antisocial behaviour in his teens. After his parents' death, his elder brother Nathan continued the practice of keeping Boo inside. He hasn't been seen in daylight for many years, but the gossips of Maycomb love to pass stories about him round the town.

The doors of the Radley house were closed on weekdays as well as Sundays, and Mr Radley's boy was not seen again for fifteen years.

But there came a day, barely within Jem's memory, when Boo Radley was heard from and was seen by several people, but not by Jem.

Jem received most of his information from Miss Stephanie Crawford, a neighbourhood scold, who said she knew the whole thing. According to Miss Stephanie, Boo was sitting in the living-room cutting some items from *The Maycomb Tribune* to paste in his scrapbook. His father entered the room. As Mr Radley passed by, Boo drove the scissors into his parent's leg, pulled them out, wiped them on his pants, and resumed his activities.

Mrs Radley ran screaming into the street that Arthur was killing them all, but when the sheriff arrived he found Boo still sitting in the living-room, cutting up the *Tribune*. He was thirty-three years old then.

The sheriff hadn't the heart to put him in jail alongside Negroes, so Boo was locked in the courthouse basement.

Boo's **transition** from the basement to back home was **nebulous** in Jem's memory. Miss Stephanie Crawford said some of the town council told Mr Radley that if he didn't take Boo back, Boo would die of mould from the damp. Besides, Boo could not live forever on the bounty of the county.

Nobody knew what form of intimidation Mr Radley employed to keep Boo out of sight, but Jem figured that Mr Radley kept him chained to the bed most of the time. Atticus said no, it wasn't that sort of thing, that there were other ways of making people into ghosts.

passage from one place to another

cloudy

- 'The sheriff hadn't the heart to put him in jail alongside Negros'. What does this tell us about attitudes at the time?
- What sort of person is Miss Stephanie Crawford?
- Can you imagine the result of being isolated and deprived of freedom for many years? What ways of 'making people into ghosts' might Atticus be thinking of?

Dill's curiosity about Boo grows and Jem feeds the legend. The children enjoy frightening themselves with their own living ghost.

Dill wants to make Boo come out and dares Jem to go and get him. He taunts Jem with being too scared. Dill keeps this up for three days ...

Folks in Meridian certainly aren't as afraid as the folks in Maycomb.

He'll kill us each and every one ... Don't blame me when he gouges your eyes out. You started it, remember.

I won't say you ran out on a dare if you just go up and touch the house.

He'll probably come out after you when he sees you in the yard, then Scout 'n' me'll jump on him and hold him down till we can tell him we ain't gonna hurt him.

Well go on.

I'm going, don't hurry me.

... as we stared we thought we saw an inside shutter move. Flick. A tiny, almost invisible movement, and the house was still.

- How does Dill move the game forward and save Jem from losing face?

- The children have lost all sense of Boo being a real person. What has Boo become in the children's minds?

Summer ends, Dill has to go back to Meridian and Scout starts school. Scout has her first encounter with a world that doesn't make sense. Miss Caroline Fisher is new to teaching and new to southern Alabama.

Does anybody know what these are?

All the class know the alphabet. Miss Fisher discovers that Scout can read fluently. She has been taught by Atticus. Calpurnia has taught her to write. This doesn't fit in with the way Miss Fisher wants to do things and she is annoyed.

Tell him I'll take over from here. Your father doesn't know how to teach.

Miss Fisher is further annoyed by Scout when she tries to explain why Walter Cunningham is refusing to borrow money from Miss Fisher so he can have some lunch.

Walter's one of the Cunninghams, Miss Caroline ... They don't have much, but they get along on it.

You're shamin' him, Miss.

Go on and tell her, Scout.

- Scout is in trouble for being advanced in reading and writing!
- Do you think the teacher knows all the families in the area – who has enough to eat, who goes hungry, who goes barefoot by choice, who has no shoes? Does she understand the difference between the farming and town communities?
- It's Scout's first day at school, yet the rest of the class urge her to be spokesman. Why might that be?

'Not in money,' Atticus said, 'but before the year's out I'll have been paid. You watch.'

We watched. One morning Jem and I found a load of stove-wood in the back yard. Later, a sack of **hickory nuts** appeared on the back steps. With Christmas came a crate of **smilax** and holly. That spring when we found a croker-sack full of turnip greens, Atticus said Mr Cunningham had more than paid him.

nuts similar to walnuts

a root from which a drink can be made

'The Cunninghams are country folks, farmers, and **the crash** hit them hardest.'

the Wall Street Crash (1929), the collapse of America's economy; Wall Street is the financial district/stock exchange in New York

Atticus said professional people were poor because the farmers were poor. As Maycomb County was farm country, nickels and dimes were hard to come by for doctors and dentists and lawyers.

As the Cunninghams had no money to pay a lawyer, they simply paid us with what they had. 'Did you know,' said Atticus, 'that Dr Reynolds works the same way? He charges some folks a bushel of potatoes for delivery of a baby.'

Scout tries to convey this system of payment to Miss C.

'Walter hasn't got a quarter at home to bring you, and you can't use any stovewood.'

Miss Caroline stood stock still, then grabbed me by the collar and hauled me back to her desk. 'Jean Louise, I've had about enough of you this morning,' she said. 'You're starting off on the wrong foot in every way, my dear. Hold out your hand.'

I thought she was going to spit in it, which was the only reason anybody in Maycomb held out his hand; it was a time-honoured method of sealing **oral contracts**. Wondering what bargain we had made, I turned to the class for an answer, but the class looked back at me in puzzlement. Miss Caroline picked up her ruler, gave me half a dozen quick little pats, then told me to stand in the corner. A storm of laughter broke loose when it finally occurred to the class that Miss Caroline had whipped me.

spoken agreements

- In the Wall Street Crash, America's finances were wrecked, which led to the 'Great Economic Depression' and created great poverty in America, and then in Europe.

- How has the Depression affected Maycomb?

At lunchtime, Scout feels that Walter Cunningham has been a major contributor to her problems with her teacher. She is dealing with him in her usual way, when Jem stops her.

Stop ... you're bigger'n he is ...

He's as old as you, nearly. He made me start off on the wrong foot.

Why?

He didn't have any lunch.

Come on home to dinner with us ... We'd be glad to have you.

They pass the Radley house, confident because there are three of them.

I went all the way up to the house once.

Anybody who went up to the house once ought not to still run every time he passes it.

- Jem is chatting to Walter, putting him at his ease. What is Scout doing?
- What words would you use to describe Scout? Remember this is her first day at school.

- 'He didn't have any lunch.' This is not a logical reason to fight someone! But, to six-year-old Scout, it makes perfect sense.

9

Walter shows his maturity in discussing farming with Atticus; then a difference in customs has Scout in trouble again. She learns an important lesson from Atticus and from Calpurnia who share the same ideas on correct behaviour.

Reason I can't pass the first grade, Mr Finch, is I've had to stay out ever' spring an' help Papa with the choppin', but there's another'n at the house now that's **field size**.

Any molasses in the house?

... he's gone and drowned his dinner in syrup ... he's poured it all over.

That boy's **yo' comp'ny** and if he wants to eat up the tablecloth you let him.

Anybody sets foot in this house's yo' comp'ny, and don't you let me catch you remarkin' on their ways.

field size – big enough to work
yo' comp'ny – your guest

- Why does Calpurnia think Scout has been ill-mannered?
- How many times has Scout been in trouble before afternoon school?
- How many times has she deserved to be in trouble?

Miss Caroline displays her ignorance of the community yet again and is rescued by little Chuck, an undersized child from a poor farming family and by the kindness of the other children.

cootie – head louse
lye soap – antiseptic/carbolic soap

• What words describe little Chuck? Do you see any similarities to Jem?

11

Burris Ewell is nine. He is big for his age, ragged, filthy and aggressive.

One of the older children explains that all the Ewell children only turn up on the first day to enrol, then are absent for the rest of the year.

paw's right contentious – father is very bad-tempered/argumentative

- How much chance do you think Burris has of learning how to behave?
- Miss Caroline is learning – she is ready to listen to the explanation of 'he's a Ewell'. Compare it to her reaction to 'he's one of the Cunninghams' on page 7.

Little Chuck comes to the rescue again.

You try and make me.

Let him go, ma'am. He's a mean one, a hard-down mean one. He's liable to start somethin'.

I'd soon's kill you as look at you. Now go home.

... be damned to ye! Ain't no snot-nosed slut of a schoolteacher ever born c'n make me do nothin'! You ain't makin' me go nowhere, missus. You just remember that, you ain't makin' me go nowhere!

When Burris is sure Miss Caroline is crying, he leaves.

... he was a real mean one.

... them ain't Maycomb's ways.

...below the belt.

... why don't you read us a story?

... now don't you fret, ma'am.

- What do you think of the way Burris talks to Miss Caroline?
- Little Chuck and many of the other children come from underprivileged homes, yet they are kind and decent.
- How much of Burris Ewell's character comes from his character (nature) and how much from the way he has been brought up, the examples set at home (nurture)?
- What do you think Scout's impression might be of this first encounter with a Ewell?

13

Scout goes home after her first eventful day at school. She thinks Walter Cunningham, Atticus and Calpurnia all got her into trouble at school, then Atticus and Calpurnia were angry with her at lunchtime. 'Weary with the day's crimes', Scout is not ready to forgive Calpurnia and doesn't want to read as usual with her father.

Cal has made a treat for Scout – her favourite crackling bread.

Shut your eyes and open your mouth. I missed you today.

Something wrong, Scout?

You never went to school and you do all right, so I'll just stay home too.

Bit by bit, Scout told Atticus the day's misfortunes.

First of all, if you can learn a simple trick, Scout, you'll get along a lot better with all kinds of folks. You never really understand a person until you consider things from his point of view – until you climb into his skin and walk around in it.

...and she said you taught me all wrong, so we can't ever read any more, ever. Please don't send me back.

Atticus points out that Scout has learned many things in school that day and if she put herself in Miss Caroline's shoes, she would see she had made honest mistakes. Miss Caroline couldn't learn all Maycomb's ways in one day or be held responsible for them when she knew no better.

'I'll be dogged,' I said. 'I didn't know no better than not to read to her, and she held me responsible – listen, Atticus, I don't have to go to school!' I was bursting with a sudden thought. 'Burris Ewell, remember? He just goes to school the first day. The truant lady reckons she's carried out the law when she gets his name on the roll–'

'You can't do that, Scout,' Atticus said. 'Sometimes it's better to bend the law a little in special cases. In your case, the law remains rigid. So to school you must go.'

Atticus said the Ewells had been the disgrace of Maycomb for three generations. None of them had done an honest day's work in his recollection. He said that some Christmas, when he was getting rid of the tree, he would take me with him and show me where and how they lived. They were people, but they lived like animals. 'They can go to school any time they want to, when they show the faintest symptom of wanting an education,' said Atticus. 'There are ways of keeping them in school by force, but it's silly to force people like the Ewells into a new environment–'

He said that the Ewells were members of an exclusive society made up of Ewells. In certain circumstances the common folk judiciously allowed them certain privileges by the simple method of becoming blind to some of the Ewells' activities. They didn't have to go to school, for one thing. Another thing, Mr Bob Ewell, Burris's father, was permitted to hunt and trap out of season.

'Atticus, that's bad,' I said. In Maycomb County, hunting out of season was a **misdemeanour** at law, a capital **felony** in the eyes of the **populace**.

misconduct/bad behaviour
serious crime
all the local community

'It's against the law, all right,' said my father, 'and it's certainly bad, but when a man spends his relief cheques on green whisky his children have a way of crying from hunger pains. I don't know of any landowner around here who begrudges those children any game their father can hit.'

'Mr Ewell shouldn't do that–'

'Of course he shouldn't, but he'll never change his ways. Are you going to take out your disapproval on his children?'

- Scout is quick to see how Atticus's argument can be used to her advantage.

- Atticus is a believer in, and an upholder of, the law but can see when it is more humane to turn a blind eye.
- Why is there one rule for Scout and another for Burris?

Scout is still bothered by the reading problem, so Atticus teaches her about compromise and makes a deal with her.

Do you know what a compromise is?

Bending the law?

No ... it works this way. If you'll **concede** the necessity of going to school, we'll go on reading every night just as we always have. Is it a bargain?

Yes sir.

Scout prepares to spit on her hand to seal the bargain.

We'll consider it sealed without the usual formality.

By the way, Scout, you'd better not say anything at school about our agreement.

Why not?

I have a feeling that if you tell Miss Caroline ... she'll get after me, and I wouldn't want her after me.

concede – agree to

- Atticus has dealt with Scout's unhappiness with understanding and humour. He has also got her to agree to returning to school.

- How many things has Atticus taught Scout since she got home?
- Would Burris Ewell be treated the same way if he went home feeling troubled?

Scout continues to go to school and learns as much as she can at home. Scout's class leaves thirty minutes before Jem's, so Scout sprints past the Radley place. One day near the end of the summer term, something is glinting in the oak tree outside the Radley house …

Scout runs away with her loot as fast as possible.

Chewing gum – she sniffs it, licks it, doesn't die, so eats it.

Spit it out right now!

Don't you know you're not supposed to even touch the trees over there?

You go gargle – right now!

You'll get killed if you do!

You don't 'n I'll tell Calpurnia on you!

• The fear of Boo Radley and his house is still large in the children's minds.

• Calpurnia, like Atticus, is recognised by Jem and Scout as a figure of authority.

On the last day of term, Jem and Scout walk home from school together. They are looking forward to the arrival of Dill for the summer holidays. Then they see another shiny object in the Radley's oak tree.

I see it, Scout! I see it –

Indian-heads ... these are real old.

... you reckon that's somebody's hidin'-place?

Naw, unless it's some grown person's–

– these are important to somebody.

How's that Jem ... ?

... they come from the Indians. They're real strong magic, they make you have good luck.

Jem is thinking again.

Indian-heads – coins with the heads of Native American Indians on one side

 • What might Jem be thinking as he looks at the Radley place?

Dill arrives, full of wild tales about his journey and wilder ones about his father, who he claims to have met. Jem and Scout don't believe a word he says. They are used to Dill and his flights of imagination, and start thinking up some new games for the summer.

Scout crams herself into the tyre and Jem gives her an extra big push to set the tyre rolling – faster than usual. The tyre rolls straight into the Radley yard.

Scout, get away from there.

... don't just lie there! Get up, can'tcha?

Chuckle chuckle

Calpurnia calls them out of the sun for some lemonade.

I know what we are going to play ... Boo Radley.

Scout is afraid that Boo will find out about their Boo Radley game and come after them. Jem says Boo is already dead and has been stuffed up the chimney. They both accuse Scout of being too scared, so naturally she joins in. They make strange plays based on local gossip, legend and fantasy about Boo and his family.

- The boundaries between fantasy and reality are now thoroughly blurred. The children start with fact – Boo is kept in the house. Then there is inaccurate gossip. Then they invent things, to make the gossip more interesting. This becomes fantasy, a long way from the factual starting point.

- Have you ever experienced anything like this? Think of some newspaper stories.
- Why would Atticus be cross with them for playing 'Boo Radley'?
- Who could have been laughing in the Radley house?

The Boo Radley game is now no longer popular. Relationships are changing between the three of them, they are a year older and the boys want to be off doing 'boy things', without a girl tagging along. Miss Maudie, neighbour and long-standing friend of the Finch family, fills the gap made in Scout's life.

Dill was becoming something of a trial anyway, following Jem about. He had asked me earlier in the summer to marry him, then he promptly forgot about it. He staked me out, marked as his property, said I was the only girl he would ever love, then he neglected me. I beat him up twice but it did no good, he only grew closer to Jem. They spent days together in the treehouse plotting and planning, calling me only when they needed a third party. But I kept aloof from their more foolhardy schemes for a while, and on pain of being called a g-irl, I spent most of the remaining twilights that summer sitting with Miss Maudie Atkinson on her front porch.

Miss Maudie hated her house: time spent indoors was time wasted. She was a widow, a chameleon lady who worked in her flower-beds in an old straw hat and men's coveralls, but after her five o'clock bath she would appear on the porch and reign over the street in **magisterial** beauty.

with the air of authority

She loved everything that grew in God's earth, even the weeds. Her speech was crisp for a Maycomb County inhabitant. She called us by all our names, and when she grinned she revealed two minute gold prongs clipped to her eye-teeth. When I admired them and hoped I would have some eventually, she said, 'Look here.' With a click of her tongue she thrust out her bridgework, a gesture of **cordiality** that cemented our friendship.

hospitality
kindness

Miss Maudie's **benevolence** extended to Jem and Dill, whenever they paused in their pursuits: we reaped the benefits of a talent Miss Maudie had hitherto kept hidden from us. She made the best cakes in the neighbourhood. When she was admitted into our confidence, every time she baked she made a big cake and three little ones, and she would call across the street: 'Jem Finch, Scout Finch, Charles Baker Harris, come here!' Our promptness was always rewarded.

In summertime, twilights are long and peaceful. Often as not, Miss Maudie and I would sit silently on her porch, watching the sky go from yellow to pink as the sun went down, watching flights of martins sweep low over the neighbourhood and disappear behind the schoolhouse rooftops.

Do you think Boo Radley's still alive?

His name's Arthur and he's alive.

Maybe he died and they stuffed him up the chimney.

Where did you get such a notion?

It's the last night of the summer holidays. The boys plan to creep up to the back of the Radley house after dark to peep inside. Knowing this would be forbidden, Scout protests.

Scout, I'm tellin' you for the last time, shut your trap or go home ... You're gettin' more like a girl every day!

- Although Scout is good at thinking things out, she still has to check with a trusted adult when fantasy and reality are hard to separate.

- Where *did* Scout 'get such a notion'? See page 20.

The children are terrified by the shadow of a man with a gun in the moonlight, gunshot sends them racing for home. Jem's trousers get stuck on the fence and have to be left behind.

The shot brought the neighbours out. They gathered outside the Radleys'. Scout and the boys have to join them quickly because it would look suspicious if they didn't. Having regained their breath, they stroll up, acting innocently.

What happened?

Mr Radley shot at a Negro … Shot in the air. Scared him pale, though … anybody sees a white nigger, that's …

Where're your **pants**, son?

Jem Finch!

We were playin' strip-poker up yonder by the fishpool.

Were you all playing cards?

No sir, just with matches.

I won 'em.

Won them? How?

Dill Harris! Gamblin' by my fishpool? I'll strip-poker you, sir!

They are sent to Dill's aunt's house to collect the pants and to say goodbye to Dill until next summer.

Yawl write, hear?

pants – trousers/shorts

- What section of society is blamed for any disturbance?
- Matches might be dangerous, but card playing was regarded as sinful by people like Miss Rachel (Dill's aunt)!
- How quick-thinking are the two boys?

School starts next day and Jem has no trousers! Scout is appalled that he intends to go back for them, alone, in the dark to that terrifying place. Although Jem is scared of going back, his father's good opinion is more important to him than fear of Nathan Radley's gun.

Jem returns safe and sound.

? • Jem is growing up. Are he and Scout still on the same wavelength?

• Do you think Jem is ashamed of their behaviour? If so, what aspects of it is he ashamed of?

25

Jem has become very withdrawn and thoughtful, so Scout tries 'walking around in his skin', and decides he is still suffering from the terror of going back for his trousers. It is September 1934 and school starts again. Scout now finishes school at the same time as Jem, so they can walk home together. They find more presents in the oak tree.

They find soap carvings.

These are good ... These are us.

Who did 'em, you reckon?

Chewing gum.

An old-fashioned medal.

A pocket watch and a knife on a chain.

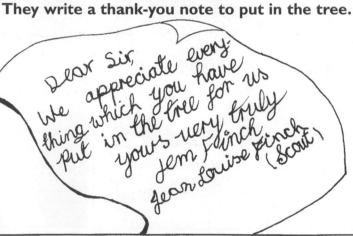

They write a thank-you note to put in the tree.

Dear Sir,
We appreciate every-thing which you have put in the tree for us
yours very truly
Jem Finch
Jean Louise Finch
(Scout)

- What assumption does Jem make about the person they are writing to?
- Have you any ideas who it might be?

Next morning, they run to put the letter in the tree, but are horrified to find the hole cemented up. At lunchtime Jem lays in wait for Mr Nathan Radley, Boo's elder brother, who 'looks after' Boo.

Did you put cement in that hole?

Yes.

Why'd you do it?

Tree's dying. You plug 'em when they're sick.

Is that tree dyin'?

Why, no son. Look at the leaves ... That tree's as healthy as you are.

Scout sees something new.

The *world's* endin', Atticus! Please do something—!

No it's not. It's snowing.

The first snow in Maycomb since 1895! Jem and Scout only have a small amount of soggy snow. Quick-thinking Jem makes an excellent figure with the dark earth, and then they coat it with the white snow ...

From now on I'll never worry about what'll become of you, son, you'll always have an idea.

- Why do you think Nathan Radley has cemented up the hole in the tree?
- The snowman is part dark brown and part white. What do you think the two colours might represent?

The wooden houses of Alabama were not built to conserve heat. Miss Maudie stoked her fire overnight to keep her young plants safe and warm. The dry old house caught fire. The whole neighbourhood turns out in the freezing cold to watch and help. When they are sure the fire is under control and not going to spread, they return home.

Scout notices a strange blanket around her shoulders.

He coulda cut my throat but he tried to mend my pants ... he ain't ever hurt us.

Someday, maybe Scout can thank him.

Boo Radley. You were so busy looking at the fire you didn't know it when he put the blanket around you.

Thank who?

Miss Maudie doesn't mind her big house burning down, she can build a smaller one and have a bigger garden! Meanwhile she moves in with Miss Stephanie Crawford. Jem and Scout have new trouble to deal with.

Scout Finch's daddy defends niggers!

Do you defend niggers, Atticus?

Of course I do. Don't say nigger, Scout.

's what everyone at school says.

From now on it'll be everybody less one.

 • Jem has realised their invisible neighbour is not a monster at all. He may be strange, but he is kind.

• In the southern states of America in the 1930s, racism and segregation were the norm. How would we react to the use of the word 'nigger' now?

> **Atticus gives Scout an idea of the trouble that lays ahead and she gets her first glimpse of a world which is not fair and sometimes very ugly.**

Atticus sighed. 'I'm simply defending a Negro – his name's Tom Robinson. He lives in that little settlement beyond the town dump. He's a member of Calpurnia's church, and Cal knows his family well. She says they're clean-living folks. Scout, you aren't old enough to understand some things yet, but there's been some high talk around town to the effect that I shouldn't do much about defending this man. It's a peculiar case – it won't come to trial until summer session. John Taylor was kind enough to give us a postponement …'

'If you shouldn't be defendin' him, then why are you doin' it?'

'For a number of reasons,' said Atticus. 'The main one is, if I didn't I couldn't hold up my head in town, I couldn't represent this country in the **legislature**, I couldn't even tell you or Jem not to do something again.'

> the body of people who make the laws

'You mean if you didn't defend that man, Jem and me wouldn't have to **mind** you anymore?'

> listen to/take notice of

'That's about right.'

'Why?'

'Because I could never ask you to mind me again. Scout, simply by the nature of the work, every lawyer gets at least one case in his lifetime that affects him personally. This one's mine, I guess. You might hear some ugly talk about it at school, but do one thing for me if you will: you just hold your head high and keep those fists down. No matter what anyone says to you, don't you let 'em get your goat. Try fighting with your head for a change … it's a good one, even if it does resist learning.'

'Atticus, are we going to win it?'

'No, honey.'

'Then why–'

'Come here, Scout,' said Atticus. I crawled into his lap and tucked my head under his chin. He put his arms around me and rocked me gently …

'Remember this, no matter how bitter things get, they're still our friends and this is still our home.'

- What does Atticus mean by 'fighting with your head'?

- Atticus is saying if you believe something is right, you must stand by it against all odds, if you don't you lose your self-respect – 'I couldn't hold my head up.'

Christmas arrives, and so does Uncle Jack. He is Atticus's younger brother, a doctor and a great favourite with Scout and Jem. On Christmas Day they all have to go to Finch's Landing to join the family. That means Aunt Alexandra and, even worse, Cousin Francis, who is one year older than Scout.

• What words could you use to describe Uncle Jack?
• What sort of relationship does he have with Scout?

• Scout knows Atticus has objected to words she has learned at school. What do you think her latest game is to get out of school?

Christmas morning, and the two long parcels are air rifles. Just what the children had asked for – Atticus had asked Jack to get them. Scout and Jem are dragged away from their guns to join the family at Finch's Landing.

What'd you get for Christmas?

Scout struggles to be polite to Cousin Francis.

Knee-pants, a red leather booksack, five shirts and an untied bow-tie.

Jem and me got air rifles, and Jem got a chemistry set.

Francis starts on Atticus.

Grandma says it's bad enough he lets you all run wild, but now he's turned out a nigger-lover.

Nigger-lover!

Nigger-lover!

Nothing to speak of.

You still mad, Jean Louise?

• What do the different presents tell you about the interests and lifestyle of the two children?

• Where do you think Francis has got this information?

The fight brings Uncle Jack and Aunt Alexandra to the scene: Francis lies and says Scout started it, saying she called him a '**whore**–lady'. This confirms Aunt Alexandra's opinion that Scout is growing up wild, and Uncle Jack is very angry about the bad language. When they get back home, Uncle Jack wants to make peace.

KNOCK KNOCK

Go away!

You ain't fair … you never stopped to gimme a chance to tell you my side of it. Atticus doesn't ever just listen to Jem's side of it, he hears mine too.

What was your side of it, Scout?

Francis called Atticus somethin'. A nigger-lover … an' a lot more.

Alexandra should know about this … Wait'll I get my hands on that boy …

Uncle Jack, please promise me somethin', please sir. Promise you won't tell Atticus about this. He – he asked me one time not to let anything I heard about him make me mad, an' I'd ruther him think we were fightin' about somethin' else instead. Please promise …

Uncle Jack … what's a whore-lady?

whore – prostitute

- Scout is mature enough to feel she has betrayed Atticus's trust. How?
- What shows us that Scout is still very much a child?

'Bad language is a stage all children go through, and it dies with time when they learn they're not attracting attention with it. Hot-headedness isn't. Scout's got to learn to keep her head and learn soon, with what's in store for her these next few months.'

'Atticus, you've never laid a hand on her.'

'I admit that. So far I've been able to get by with threats. Jack, she minds me as well as she can. Doesn't come up to scratch half the time, but she tries ... she knows I know she tries. That's what makes the difference. What bothers me is that she and Jem will have to absorb some ugly things pretty soon. I'm not worried about Jem keeping his head, but Scout'd just as soon jump on someone as look at him if her pride's at stake ...'

I waited for Uncle Jack to break his promise. He still didn't.

'Atticus, how bad is this going to be? You haven't had too much chance to discuss it.'

'It couldn't be worse, Jack. The only thing we've got is a black man's word against the Ewells'. The evidence boils down to you – did – I – didn't. The jury couldn't possibly be expected to take Tom Robinson's word against the Ewells'.

'What are you going to do, then?'

'Before I'm through, I intend to jar the jury a bit – I think we'll have a reasonable chance on appeal, though. You know what's going to happen as well as I do, Jack, and I hope and I pray I can get Jem and Scout through it without bitterness, and most of all, without catching Maycomb's usual disease. Why reasonable people go stark raving mad when anything involving a Negro comes up, is something I don't pretend to understand ... I just hope that Jem and Scout come to me for their answers instead of listening to the town. I hope they trust me enough. ... Jean Louise?'

My scalp jumped. I stuck my head around the corner. 'Sir?'

'Go to bed.'

Uncle Jack was a prince of a fellow not to let me down. But I never figured out how Atticus knew I was listening, and it was not until many years later that I realized he wanted me to hear every word he said.

- Atticus understands his daughter very well. What shows us how clever he is at managing her?
- Is Atticus expecting to win his case?
- What does Atticus mean by 'Maycomb's usual disease'?

Atticus had refused to teach the children how to use their guns and made Uncle Jack teach them. Scout reflects on their father's shortcomings – how he won't play football, go hunting, play poker, drink and smoke like other fathers. He is also causing them a lot of grief at school by defending Tom Robinson.

Your father's right. Mockingbirds don't do one thing but make music for us to enjoy. They don't eat up people's gardens, don't nest in corncribs, they don't do one thing but sing their hearts out for us. That's why it's a sin to kill a mockingbird.

I'd rather you shot at tin cans, but I know you'll go after birds … remember it's a sin to kill a mockingbird.

Later, the children see a dog they know approaching them. It is behaving strangely.

Calpurnia alerts the neighbours, and they all get inside and shut their doors.

Heck Tate and Atticus arrive, Heck carries a gun.

Not runnin', is he?

I'm gonna tell Cal.

Mad dog's comin'.

Naw sir, he's in the twitchin' stage.

- Have you any ideas yet about the title of the book? Think of Miss Maudie's description. Is there anyone so far who is ill-treated, although they do no one any harm?

- Rabies (hydrophobia) is a disease in dogs that turns them 'mad' in the final stages, when their bite can kill a human.

Jem and Scout look out on a deserted waiting street. The trees are still, the mockingbirds silent. Only Atticus and the sheriff are out there with the rabid dog. Jem and Scout learn something about their father.

Take him, Mr Finch.

This is a one-shot job.

For God's sake, look where he is! Miss and you'll go straight into the Radley house! I can't shoot that well.

I haven't shot a gun in thirty years.

With movements so swift they seemed simultaneous, Atticus's hand yanked a ball-tipped lever as he brought the gun to his shoulder. The rifle cracked. Tim Johnson leaped, flopped over and crumpled on the sidewalk in a brown-and-white heap. He didn't know what hit him.

D'you see him?

All of a sudden he just relaxed all over ... looked like that gun was a part of him.

So quick.

Atticus Finch was the deadest shot in Maycomb County in his time.

I guess he decided he wouldn't shoot till he had to, and he had to today.

Tim Johnson – the dog's name was Tim, and the custom was to give the family name, as well

- Atticus doesn't want to use the gun, so why does he?
- What have the children learned about their father?

The day after Jem's 12th birthday, Jem and Scout go into town to spend his birthday money. They pass Mrs Dubose's house and the angry old lady shouts abuse and insults as usual; this day she goes too far. On the way back, Jem takes his revenge …

He smashes the heads of all her camellias.

Jem is sent to apologise. His punishment is to read to her every afternoon after school. Scout goes with him for moral support. An alarm clock is set when they arrive, and the bell means they can go. The time gets longer every day …

So you brought that dirty little sister of yours.

One evening, Atticus is called to Mrs Dubose. On his return, he tells the children she is dead.

Mrs Dubose was a morphine addict. She took it as a painkiller for years. The doctor put her on it. She said she was going to leave this world **beholden to** nothing.

You mean that's what her fits were?

Most of the time you were reading to her I doubt if she heard a word you said. Her whole mind and body were concentrated on that alarm clock.

I wanted you to see what real courage is, instead of getting the idea that courage is a man with a gun in his hand. She was the bravest person I ever knew.

beholden to – owing/indebted to

● Why did Mrs Dubose want to bear the pain rather than die addicted to morphine?
● How did Jem and Scout help her?
● Can you describe what Atticus believes to be real courage?

Part Two

Summer comes. Jem wants to be off playing football and Dill has a new father and is staying in Meridian. Scout spends more time with Calpurnia in the kitchen and she has to admit there is some skill in being a girl. Atticus is away for two weeks, and Cal decides to take them to her church on Sunday.

I don't want anybody sayin' I don't look after my children.

Mister Jem, you absolutely can't wear that tie with that suit.

Only one person objects.

You ain't got no business bringin' white chillun here.

It's the same God, ain't it?

They are led to the front pew by the Reverend Sykes.

Brethren and sisters, we are particularly glad to have company. You all know their father.

The faith is strong and practical. Hymns and prayers are conducted by 'linin' – one person reads and sings out the line, then the congregation sings it back with harmonies. The sound is beautiful. They do it this way because there is no money for hymn books and anyway most people can't read.

Money is collected from the congregation for particular purposes. Today they must dig deep for Tom Robinson's wife, Helen, and their children.

- Writing is not the only thing Calpurnia can teach Scout. What else might she learn?
- How does Calpurnia regard Jem and Scout?

- What sort of reception do you think two black children would have received in a white church in Alabama at this time?

On the way home, the children question Cal, and discover that Tom Robinson is accused by Bob Ewell of raping his daughter. Even though the Ewells are known as **trash**, no one will side with a black man against a white man. They also discover Cal was born at Finch's Landing and was educated by their grandfather and Miss Maudie's aunt. They realise this explains her cultured speech, although she can speak the local negro dialect as well. Like Atticus, it seems that Cal has a history and abilities they knew nothing about. Scout is intrigued and asks to be allowed to visit Calpurnia's home. 'Any time you want to,' says Calpurnia.

Aunt Alexandra has arrived to stay!

Put my bag in the front bedroom, Calpurnia.

Aunt Alexandra refuses to let Scout go to Calpurnia's.

You may *not*.

She tries to get rid of Calpurnia.

We don't need her now.

Calpurnia's not leaving this house until she wants to. I couldn't have got along without her all these years – and another thing, the children love her.

trash – poor, uneducated and white

- Is the world the children live in just as they imagined? How many new things have they learned so far?
- How does Aunt Alexandra's attitude to Cal differ from Atticus, Jem and Scout's?
- Why do you think their aunt has moved in? Look at pages 31–32.

Jem realises that Tom Robinson's case is 'worryin' [Atticus] to death', and asks Scout to stop antagonising their aunt. Scout is furious that now even Jem is ordering her about. A fight ensues, which confirms Aunt Alexandra's view that the children are wild. They are sent to bed early, but Scout thinks there is something under her bed, and gets Jem – it might be a snake!

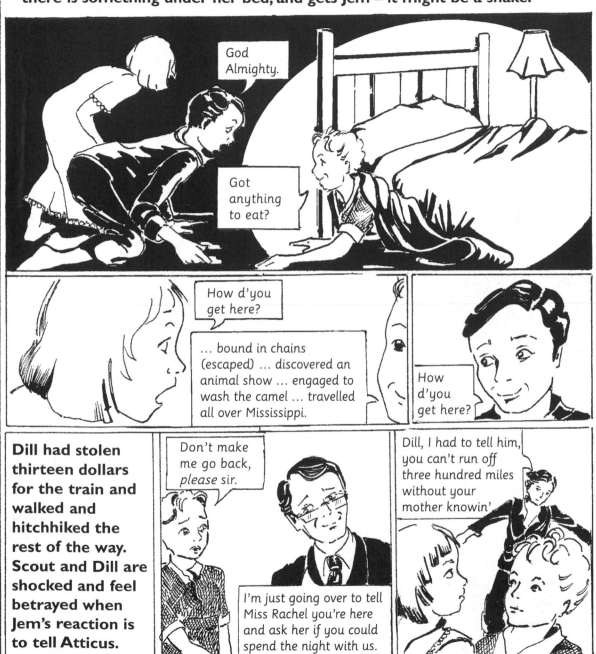

Dill had stolen thirteen dollars for the train and walked and hitchhiked the rest of the way. Scout and Dill are shocked and feel betrayed when Jem's reaction is to tell Atticus.

• How well does Jem know Dill?
• Jem has stepped away from childhood and taken responsible action.

• Why do Dill and Scout feel betrayed?

39

'That wasn't it, he – they just wasn't interested in me.'

This was the weirdest reason for flight I had ever heard.

'How come?'

'Well, they stayed gone all the time, and when they were home, even, they'd get off in a room by themselves.'

'What'd they do in there?'

'Nothin', just sittin' and readin' – but they didn't want me with 'em.'

As Dill explained, I found myself wondering what life would be if Jem were different, even from what he was now; what I would do if Atticus did not feel the necessity of my presence, help and advice. Why, he couldn't get along a day without me. Even Calpurnia couldn't get along unless I was there. They needed me.

Dill's voice went on steadily in the darkness: 'The thing is, what I'm tryin' to say is – they *do* get on a lot better without me, I can't help them any. They ain't mean. They buy me everything I want, but it's now-you've-got-it-go-play-with-it. You've got a roomful of things. I-got-you-that-book-so-go-read-it.'

Dill was off again. Beautiful things floated around in his dreamy head. He could read two books to my one, but he preferred the magic of his own inventions. He could add and subtract faster than lightning, but he preferred his own twilight world …

He was slowly talking himself to sleep and taking me with him, but in the quietness of his foggy island there rose the faded image of a grey house with sad brown doors.

'Dill?'

'Mm?'

'Why do you reckon Boo Radley's never run off?'

Dill sighed a long sigh and turned away from me.

'Maybe he doesn't have anywhere to run off to …'

- How exactly has Dill been made unhappy?
- Do you think he is right about Boo Radley?

Dill is allowed to stay with his Aunt Rachel; but this summer will not be like the others. As Scout says, 'a nightmare was upon us'. On the Saturday night before Tom's trial on the Monday, a group of men come to the house to warn Atticus. They say that on the next day – when Tom is brought to the town jail ready for his trial – an out-of-town **lynch mob** are after Tom and may harm Atticus as well.

You've got everything to lose from this, Atticus. I mean everything.

Scout ... I'm scared.

Scared'a what?

Scared about Atticus. Somebody might hurt him.

Sunday evening

You folks'll be in bed when I come back, so I'll say good night now.

Later ...

Why ain't you going to bed?

I'm goin' downtown for a while.

No way can Jem get away without Scout and Dill.

Jem's got the look-arounds.

I just got this feeling, just this feeling.

In the town square Atticus has put the extension cord to use.

lynch mob – illegal band of people determined to kill/hang someone for a crime before they have even been tried

41

Four cars arrive and a group of men surround Atticus. They have tricked the sheriff out of town and Atticus (Tom's only protector) is on his own, sitting outside the jail.

He in there?

You know what we want. Get aside from the door.

He is. You can turn around and go home.

H-ey, Atticus!

Jem ... Take Scout and Dill home.

Son, I said go home.

I'll send him home.

Don't you touch him!

Scout recognises Walter Cunningham (Senior) in the crowd and acts instinctively. She starts chattering to him about the legal work Atticus is doing for him, and about young Walter.

Everyone is staring at Scout.

What's the matter?

I'll tell him you said hey, little lady.

Let's clear out. Let's get going, boys.

- What do the men want to do?
- How does Scout change the group of men from a mob (where no one is 100 per cent responsible) back into a group of individuals who are each entirely responsible for their own actions?

Atticus reassures Tom that the mob won't be back. The four of them walk home feeling close and saying little. Next morning, the day of the trial, Atticus explains something about the make-up of a mob.

'Why don't you drink your coffee, Scout?'

I was playing in it with the spoon. 'I thought Mr Cunningham was a friend of ours. You told me a long time ago he was.'

'He still is.'

'But last night he wanted to hurt you.'

Atticus placed his fork beside his knife and pushed his plate aside. 'Mr Cunningham's basically a good man,' he said, 'he just has his blind spots along with the rest of us.'

Jem spoke. 'Don't call that a blind spot. He'da killed you last night when he first went there.'

'He might have hurt me a little,' Atticus conceded, 'but son, you'll understand folks a little better when you're older. A mob's always made up of people, no matter what. Mr Cunningham was part of a mob last night, but he was still a man. Every mob in every little Southern town is always made up of people you know – doesn't say much for them, does it?'

'I'll say not,' said Jem.

'So it took an eight-year-old to bring 'em to their senses, didn't it?' said Atticus. 'That proves something – that a gang of wild animals *can* be stopped, simply because they're still human. Hmp, maybe we need a police force of children ... you children last night made Walter Cunningham stand in my shoes for a minute. That was enough ... There's a day ahead, so excuse me. Jem, I don't want you and Scout downtown today, please.'

As Atticus departed, Dill came bounding down the hall into the dining-room. 'It's all over town this morning,' he announced, 'all about how we held off a hundred folks with our bare hands ...'

Aunt Alexandra stared him to silence. 'It was not a hundred folks,' she said, 'and nobody held anybody off. It was just a nest of those Cunninghams, drunk and disorderly.'

'Aw, Aunty, that's just Dill's way,' said Jem. He signalled us to follow him.

'You all stay in the yard today,' she said, as we made our way to the front porch.

- Have you ever witnessed mob mentality, bullying for example, or bad behaviour in class or outside of school?

- '... stand in my shoes for a minute.' Where have you heard Atticus express the same idea before? Look at page 14.

The children are forbidden to go into town that day. They watch people from out of town streaming past their house in party mood, all heading for the courthouse and expecting entertainment.

… watching a poor devil on trial for his life. Look at all those folks, it's like a Roman carnival.

After lunch, the children can be obedient no longer. They arrive in town to find a crowd battling to get upstairs to the courtroom. The children fear they may have missed the chance of a seat.

You know the court appointed him to defend this nigger.

Yeah, but Atticus aims to defend him. That's what I don't like about it.

Whoa now, just a minute … Just don't start up them there stairs yet awhile.

Reverend Sykes takes them up to the 'Coloured' balcony. There they are welcomed, and seats are given up for them.

Do you reckon it'll be all right if you all came to the balcony with me?

Gosh yes.

- Why doesn't the man like the idea that Atticus is actually going to defend Tom? What might he have expected from Atticus's defence?
- If we saw someone behaving like the man with the walking stick, how would we behave?
- What does the kindness and courtesy of the black community say about their attitudes and beliefs?

Judge Taylor presides over the court. Although he seems sleepy, he is in fact sharp and perceptive. Heck Tate testifies that he was called by Bob Ewell to his daughter, Mayella. Bob Ewell said she had been beaten and raped by Tom Robinson.

Did you call a doctor, Sheriff?

... describe her injuries, Heck.

No sir.

It was her right eye... she was bunged up on that side of the face ... finger marks on her **gullet** ... all around.

Bob Ewell is called to the stand. He feels sure that his white skin will win the case.

Every town the size of Maycomb had families like the Ewells. No economic fluctuations changed their status – people like the Ewells lived as guests of the county in prosperity as well as in the depths of a depression. No truant officers could keep their numerous offspring in school; no public health officer could free them from congenital defects, various worms, and the diseases **indigenous** to filthy surroundings.

Maycomb Ewells lived behind the town garbage dump in what was once a Negro cabin ... A dirt road ran from the highway past the dump, down to a small Negro settlement some five hundred yards beyond the Ewells' ... their cabins looked neat and snug with pale blue smoke rising from the chimneys and doorways glowing amber from the fire inside. All the little man on the witness stand had that made him any better than his nearest neighbours was, that if scrubbed with lye soap in very hot water, his skin was white.

gullet – throat
indigenous to – typical of

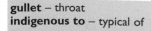

 • What do you think Atticus is trying to find out?

'You were in the courtroom when Mr Heck Tate was on the stand, weren't you? You heard everything he said, didn't you?'

Mr Ewell considered the matter carefully, and seemed to decide that the question was safe.

'Yes,' he said.

'Do you agree with his descriptions of Mayella's injuries?'

'How's that?'

'Mr Tate testified that her right eye was blackened, that she was beaten around the–'

'Oh yeah,' said the witness. 'I hold with everything Tate said … I holds with Tate. Her eye was blacked and she was mighty beat up.'

'Mr Ewell, can you read and write?'

'I most positively can.'

'Will you write your name and show us?'

'I most positively will. How do you think I sign my relief checks?'

Mr Ewell was endearing himself to his fellow citizens. The whispers and chuckles below probably had to do with what a card he was.

'You're left-handed, Mr Ewell,' said Judge Taylor.

Jem seemed to be having a quiet fit. He was pounding the balcony rail softly, and once he whispered, 'We've got him.'

I didn't think so: Atticus was trying to show, it seemed to me, that Mr Ewell could have beaten up Mayella. That much I could follow. If her right eye was blacked and she was beaten mostly on the right side of the face, it would tend to show that a left-handed person did it. But Tom Robinson could easily be left-handed, too. Like Mr Heck Tate, I imagined a person facing me, went through a swift mental pantomime, and concluded that he might have held her with his right hand and pounded her with his left. I looked down at him. His back was to us, but I could see his broad shoulders and bull-thick neck. He could easily have done it. I thought Jem was counting his chickens.

contempt of court – being disobedient or disrespectful in court

- Stand opposite somebody and touch their shoulder with your left hand. Which of their shoulders have you just touched?
- Mayella's injuries were on her right side and her father is left-handed. What is the connection?

Nineteen-year-old Mayella takes the stand. She is angry and very wary of Atticus, because she has just seen him make her father look small, although she is not sure how. She gives her evidence ... describing how she called Tom over ...

Come here, nigger.

...'fore I knew it he was on me. He hit me agin an' agin – he **chunked** me on the floor an' took advantage of me.

... Next thing I knew Papa was ... a'standin' over me hollerin' who done it ... an' the next thing I knew Mr Tate was pullin' me up offa the floor and leading me to the water-bucket.

Miss Mayella.

He keeps on callin' me ma'am an' sayin' Miss Mayella. I don't hafta take his sass.

Mr Finch is always courteous to everybody.

He's not trying to mock you.

I wondered if anyone had called her ma'am or Miss Mayella in her life.

Atticus builds up a picture of Mayella's life. Her mother is dead, she is isolated, and she cares for her seven younger brothers and sisters on very little money, because her father spends the **relief cheque** on drink. Bob Ewell is frequently drunk, and, Atticus implies, probably violent.

My paw's never touched a hair o' my head in my life.

You never asked him to do odd jobs before?

I mighta.

There was several niggers around.

chunked – threw
relief cheque – money from the government to help poorer families

chiffarobe – a wardrobe with drawers or shelves on one side

- Who do you think beat Mayella up?
- How is Mayella feeling?

Tom gives his version of events. He describes how Mayella called him into the house. Unlike Bob Ewell, Tom gives his testimony with dignity and restraint.

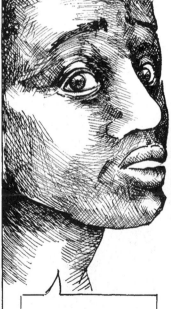

I say where the chillun? an' she says – she was laughin', sort of – she says they all gone to town to get ice-creams. She says, "Took me a slap year to save seb'm nickels, but I done it. They all gone to town."
So I done what she told me, an' I was just reachin' when the next thing I knows she – she'd grabbed me round the legs, grabbed me round th' legs, Mr Finch. She scared me so bad ... she – she hugged me. She hugged me round the waist ... She reached up an' kissed me 'side of th' face. She says she never kissed a grown man before an' she might as well kiss a nigger. She says, "Kiss me back, nigger." I say Miss Mayella lemme outa here an' tried to run but she got her back to the door an' I'da had to push her. I didn't wanta harm her, Mr Finch, an' I say lemme pass, but just when I say it Mr Ewell yonder hollered ... Somethin' not fittin' to say – not fittin' for these folks'n chillun to hear–

What did he say, Tom? You *must* tell the jury what he said.'

Tom Robinson shut his eyes tight.

He says, you goddamn whore, I'll kill ya.

Why did you run?

I was scared, suh.

Then what?

Mr Finch, I was runnin' so fast I didn't know what happened.

Why were you scared?

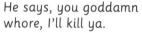

Mr Finch, if you was a nigger like me, you'd be scared, too.

• What is the answer to Atticus's question about the children? See page 48.

• Mayella has been doing some long-term planning. Why?
• Why would being a 'nigger' make Tom extra scared in this situation?

The prosecuting lawyer questions Tom. He is rude and aggressive, Tom remains polite.

Had your eye on her a long time, hadn't you, boy?

No suh, I never looked at her.

You did all this chopping and work from sheer goodness, boy? ... All this for not one penny?

Yes suh. I felt right sorry for her.

You felt sorry for her, you felt sorry for her?

The lawyer questions Tom on why he ran. He sneers at him: 'You ran, a big buck like you?'

I's scared I'd be in court, just like I am now.

Scared of arrest, scared you'd have to face up to what you did?

No suh, scared I'd hafta face up to what I didn't do.

- What is the lawyer trying to imply?
- Why might the lawyer be shocked that Tom felt sorry for Mayella?

- What does Tom mean by 'face up to what [he] didn't do'?

'She is the victim of cruel poverty and ignorance, but I cannot pity her: she is white. She knew full well the enormity of her offence, but because her desires were stronger than the code she was breaking, she persisted in breaking it. She persisted, and her subsequent reaction is something that all of us have known at one time or another. She did something every child has done – she tried to put the evidence of her offence away from her. But in this case she was no child hiding stolen contraband: she struck out at her victim – of necessity she must put him away from her – he must be removed from her presence, from this world. She must destroy the evidence of her offence.

'What was the evidence of her offence? Tom Robinson, a human being. She must put Tom Robinson away from her. Tom Robinson was a daily reminder of what she did. What did she do? She tempted a Negro.

'She was white, and she tempted a Negro. She did something that in our society is unspeakable: she kissed a black man. Not an old Uncle, but a strong young Negro man. No code mattered to her before she broke it, but it came crashing down on her afterwards.

'Her father saw it, and the defendant has testified as to his remarks. What did her father do? We don't know, but there is circumstantial evidence to indicate that Mayella Ewell was beaten savagely by someone who led almost exclusively with his left. We do know in part what Mr Ewell did: he did what any God-fearing, persevering, respectable white man would do under the circumstances – he swore out a warrant, no doubt signing it with his left hand, and Tom Robinson now sits before you, having taken the oath with the only good hand he possesses – his right hand.

'And so a quiet, respectable, humble Negro who had the **unmitigated temerity** to "feel sorry" for a white woman has had to put his word against two white people's … Gentlemen, a court is no better than each man of you sitting before me on this jury. In the name of God, do your duty.' Atticus's voice dropped. 'In the name of God, believe him.'

inexcusable cheek

- What was the rigid code that Mayella had broken?

- Atticus shows a great understanding of human nature. How does he show sympathy for Mayella?

I was past feeling: tired from fighting sleep, I allowed myself a short nap against Reverend Sykes's comfortable arm and shoulder.

Dill was sound asleep, his head on Jem's shoulder, and Jem was quiet.

But I must have been reasonably awake, or I would not have received the impression that was creeping into me. It was not unlike one I had last winter, and I shivered, though the night was hot. The feeling grew until the atmosphere in the courtroom was exactly the same as a cold February morning, when the mockingbirds were still, and the carpenters has stopped hammering on Miss Maudie's new house, and every wood door in the neighbourhood was shut as tight as the doors of the Radley Place. A deserted, waiting, empty street, and the courtroom was packed with people …

Mr Tate said, 'This court will come to order,' in a voice that rang with authority, and the heads below us jerked up.

What happened after that had a dreamlike quality: in a dream I saw the jury return, moving like underwater swimmers, and Judge Taylor's voice came from far away, and was tiny. I saw something only a lawyer's child could be expected to see, could be expected to watch for, and it was like watching Atticus walk into the street, raise a rifle to his shoulder, and pull the trigger, but watching all the time knowing that the gun was empty.

I shut my eyes. Judge Taylor was polling the jury: 'Guilty … guilty … guilty … guilty …' I peeked at Jem: his hands were white from gripping the balcony rail, and his shoulders jerked as if each 'guilty' was a separate stab between them.

'Miss Jean Louise?'

I looked around. They were standing. All around us and in the balcony on the opposite wall, the Negroes were getting to their feet. Reverend Sykes's voice was as distant as Judge Taylor's:

'Miss Jean Louise, stand up. Your father's passin'.'

- Scout remembers the tension of waiting for the mad dog's fate to be sealed, but now she feels the 'gun was empty'. What does she mean? What verdict is she expecting?
- How did Jem feel about the guilty verdict? Was he expecting it?
- How do you feel – are you surprised?
- How do the black community feel about Atticus?

They walk home together, Atticus impassive and the children sad. Jem is crying, cut by the injustice of it all. Next morning they are overwhelmed by gifts from the black community that have been left overnight.

They 'preciate what you did, Mr Finch.

Tell them I'm very grateful ... Tell them they must never do this again. Times are too hard ...

Miss Maudie offers comfort in her own way ...

Don't fret, Jem. Things are never as bad as they seem.

It's like bein' a caterpillar in a cocoon, that's what it is'. Like something asleep wrapped up in a warm place. I always thought Maycomb folks were the best in the world, least that's what they seemed like.

- Why are times so hard? See page 8.
- Tom's conviction has made Jem look at Maycomb with fresh eyes. What is he seeing?

Miss Stephanie Crawford, the neighbourhood gossip, is the first to bring the frightening news that is buzzing round town. Bob Ewell has spat in Atticus's face and threatened to get him, even if it takes him the rest of his life.

Too proud to fight, you nigger-lovin' bastard?

No, too old.

What's bothering you, son?

Mr Ewell. We're scared for you.

Jem, see if you can stand in Bob Ewell's shoes for a minute.

I destroyed his last shred of **credibility** at that trial... He had to take it out on somebody and I'd rather it be me than that houseful of children out there.

We don't have anything to fear... He got it all out of his system that morning.

I wouldn't be too sure of that ... His kind'd do anything to pay off a grudge.

credibility – feeling respected and in authority

- How did Atticus destroy Bob Ewell's credibility at the trial?
- Who do you think is right about having any more to fear from Bob Ewell – Atticus or Aunt Alexandra?

Jem and Atticus discuss the injustice of the justice system. One failing is that women in Alabama do not have the right to be jurors – so women are another group of second-class citizens! Atticus reveals something interesting about the jury's decision.

The white man always wins. They're ugly, but those are the facts of life.

Doesn't make it right.

It's all adding up and one of these days we're going to pay the bill for it.

There was one fellow who took considerable wearing down – in the beginning he was rarin' for an outright acquittal.

Who?

One of your ... friends.

One of the Cunninghams?

Although Mr Cunningham had been in the lynch mob the night before, Atticus had his reasons for allowing him on the jury.

There's no difference between one man who's going to convict and another man who's a little disturbed in his mind, isn't there? He was the only uncertainty on the whole list.

- What does this conversation tell us about the relationship between Atticus and Jem? How does he teach his children? Does he talk down to them?
- What do you think Atticus means by 'we're going to pay the bill'?
- How does Atticus show his understanding of human nature again? And how has he made use of it?

Scout wants to invite Walter over for supper and a sleepover. Aunt Alexandra tries tactfully to educate Scout into a sense of her position as a 'lady'. Then Scout's arguments push her into 'spelling it out' in a very unladylike way herself.

They're good folks. But they're not our kind of folks ... Finch women aren't interested in that sort of people.

If they're good folks why can't I be nice to Walter?

Aun-ty, she ain't nine yet.

You should be gracious to everybody, dear. But you don't have to invite him home.

But I want to play with Walter, Aunty, why can't I?

I'll tell you why.

Because – he – is – trash, that's why you can't play with him. I'll not have you around him, picking up his habits and learning Lord-knows-what.

- Most of the community are happy with their prejudice and stick rigidly to the local caste system.
- Can you think of examples of children who don't play with other children, either through choice or because they are forbidden to do so by their parents?
- Apart from Atticus, Jem and Scout, who else in the book is willing to judge people on their own merits rather than the colour of their skin or social standing?

56

Jem and Scout try to understand how the society they live in is ordered. Jem begins to see why **Boo Radley** may not want to join in with their community.

- Can you see different groups in your own community?

- What do you think Jem thinks about Boo Radley staying in his house?

'Cal,' Atticus said, 'I want you to go with me out to Helen Robinson's house–'

'What's the matter?' Aunt Alexandra asked, alarmed by the look on my father's face.

'Tom's dead.'

Aunt Alexandra put her hands to her mouth.

'They shot him,' said Atticus. 'He was running. It was during their exercise period. They said he just broke into a blind raving charge at the fence and started climbing over. Right in front of them– … Seventeen bullet holes in him. They didn't have to shoot him that much. Cal, I want you to come out with me and help me tell Helen.'

'Yes sir,' she murmured, fumbling at her apron. Miss Maudie went to Calpurnia and untied it.

Atticus leaned against the refrigerator, pushed up his glasses, and rubbed his eyes. 'We had such a good chance,' he said. 'I told him what I thought, but I couldn't in truth say that we had more than a good chance. I guess Tom was tired of white men's chances and preferred to take his own. Ready, Cal?'

Aunt Alexandra sat down in Calpurnia's chair and put her hands to her face.

Her voice rose: 'It tears him to pieces. He doesn't show it much, but it tears him to pieces. I've seen him when – what else do they want from him, Maudie, what else? Whether Maycomb knows it or not, we're paying the highest tribute we can pay a man. We trust him to do right. It's that simple.'

'Who?' Aunt Alexandra never knew she was echoing her twelve-year-old nephew.

'The handful of people in this town who say that fair play is not marked White Only; the handful of people who say a fair trial is for everybody, not just us.'

- Was Atticus hoping for a successful appeal against the verdict?

- Do you think Atticus even notices Calpurnia's colour? He trusts her with his children and turns to her for support in a time of crisis.

Miss Maudie says there is just a handful of people in Maycomb who want to see fair play. Mr Underwood, the newspaper editor, is one of them. He writes an editorial in which he 'likened Tom's death to the senseless slaughter of songbirds by hunters and children'. This gives Scout food for thought.

School starts again and Scout is still worried by Bob Ewell's threats towards Atticus. Scout says 'the events of the summer hung over us like smoke in a closed room'. Scout's new teacher is discussing current affairs.

• Look at page 34. What does Atticus say is a sin?
• Why does Mr Underwood say what he does about Tom's death?

Scout answers the question, an observation is made on the persecution of the Jews and Scout goes home with a lot to think about.

'Equal rights for all, special privileges for none.'

Very good, Jean Louise. Over here we don't believe in persecuting anybody. Persecution comes from people who are prejudiced.

Why don't they like the Jews?

I don't know. They contribute to every society they live in, and most of all, they are a deeply religious people.

One of the boys is puzzled.

They're supposed to change money or somethin', but that ain't no cause to persecute 'em. They're white, ain't they?

Later Scout is troubled about the lesson. She tells Jem about it, and then about something she overheard at the trial.

Well, coming out of the courthouse that night Miss Gates she was talking with Miss Stephanie Crawford. I heard her say it's time somebody taught 'em a lesson, they were gettin' way above themselves, an' the next thing they think they can do is marry us. Jem, how can you hate Hitler so bad an' then turn around and be ugly about folks right at home–

- What sort of people does the puzzled boy think it's normal to persecute?
- Would you say that the black community of Maycomb is hard-working and deeply religious, like the Jews? What else do they have in common?
- Do you think people always know when they are being prejudiced?
- Can you answer Scout's question to Jem?

Tom was not forgotten by his employer, Mr Link Deas. Mr Link Deas made a job for Helen … Calpurnia said it was hard on Helen, because she had to walk nearly a mile out of her way to avoid the Ewells, who, according to Helen, '**chunked at her**' the first time she tried to use the public road … Mr Link closed his store, put his hat firmly on his head, and walked Helen home. He walked her the short way, by the Ewells'. On his way back, Mr Link stopped at the crazy gate.

threw things at her, possibly stones

'Ewell?' he called. 'I say Ewell!'

'I know every last one of you's in there a-layin' on the floor! Now hear me, Bob Ewell: if I hear one more peep outa my girl Helen about not bein' able to walk this road I'll have you in jail before sundown!' Mr Link spat in the dust and walked home.

Helen went to work the next morning and used the public road. Nobody chunked at her, but when she was a few yards beyond the Ewell house, she looked around and saw Mr Ewell walking behind her. She turned and walked on, and Mr Ewell kept the same distance behind her until she reached Mr Link Deas's house. All the way to the house, Helen said, she heard a soft voice behind her, crooning foul words. Thoroughly frightened, she telephoned Mr Link at his store, which was not too far from his house. As Mr Link came out of his store he saw Mr Ewell leaning on the fence.

'First thing you can do, Ewell, is get your stinkin' carcass off my property. You're leanin' on it an' I can't afford fresh paint for it. Second thing you can do is stay away from my cook or I'll have you up for assault–'

*   *   *

'I don't like it, Atticus, I don't like it at all,' was Aunt Alexandra's assessment of these events. 'That man seems to have a permanent running grudge against everybody connected with that case. I know how that kind are about paying off grudges … Why should he try to burgle John Taylor's house?'

 • Bob Ewell, like most bullies, is a coward – he takes his anger out on Helen Robinson. Why?   • Why do you think Ewell tried to burgle the judge's house?

Halloween approaches and the Maycomb ladies, led by Mrs Merriweather, decide to keep the children out of mischief by organising games and a pageant at the school. The pageant will celebrate Maycomb County and its produce – represented by children in costume. Scout is to celebrate pork, and will be dressed as a ham!

Atticus and Aunt Alexandra are unable to attend, so Scout gives them a preview. Jem gives Scout her cue and she enters.

Jem escorts Scout to school. It's still warm, but very, very dark.

Scout waits for her cue in the wings with the other children. Mrs Merriweather drones on about Maycomb and its history. Scout is soon asleep.

Scout misses her cue.

Scout arrives late on stage, just as Mrs Merriweather is at the serious and moving end to her speech. The audience are hysterical with laughter.

Scout is totally humiliated when she realises all the laughing and clapping was largely because of her mis-timed entrance. Scout can't face anybody and wants to stay hidden inside her costume and leave after everyone else. Jem, kind and understanding, agrees. They set off in dark across the school yard.

I forgot my shoes.

Hush a minute, Scout ... Thought I heard something.

Jem, are you tryin' to scare me?

I hear it when we're walkin' along, but when we stop I don't hear it.

He said softly, 'Scout, can you take that thing off?'
'I think so, but I ain't got anything on under it much.'
'Okay,' he said, 'never mind.'
'Jem, are you afraid?'
'No. Think we're almost to the tree now.' ...
Our company shuffled and dragged his feet, as if wearing heavy shoes. Whoever it was wore thick cotton pants; what I thought were trees rustling was the soft swish of cotton on cotton, wheek, wheek, with every step.
I felt the sand go cold under my feet and I knew we were near the big oak. Jem pressed my head. We stopped and listened. Shuffle-foot had not stopped with us this time. His trousers swished softly and steadily. Then they stopped. He was running, running towards us with no child's steps.

They are attacked, and a desperate fight in the dark follows. Scout is crushed in her chicken-wire ham. Jem fights free and tries to pull Scout to the road.

I felt Jem's hand leave me, felt him jerk backwards to the ground. More scuffling, and there came a dull crunching sound and Jem screamed.

I ran in the direction of Jem's scream and sank into a flabby male stomach. Its owner said 'Uff!' and tried to catch my arms, but they were tightly **pinioned**. His stomach was soft but his arms were like steel. He slowly squeezed the breath out of me. I could not move. Suddenly he was jerked backwards and flung to the ground, almost carrying me with him. I thought, Jem's up.

Jem, Jem, help me Jem!

pinioned – held

64

Scout is stunned. There is silence apart from someone breathing heavily and staggering. She slowly realises that there is a fourth person there in the dark.

She sees a man under the street light, staggering under the weight of Jem's limp body.

Call Dr Reynolds! Where's Scout?

Here she is.

Get me the sheriff, please.

Atticus, is Jem dead?

No, Scout. Look after her, sister.

Aunty, is Jem dead?

No – no, darling, he's unconscious. Jean Louise, what happened?

I don't know.

- Aunt Alexandra has called Scout 'darling'. What does that show us about her feelings for her (underneath all the nagging)?

- Who do you think the second man might be?

Dr Reynolds arrives. He checks Scout. She has cuts and bruises and is still dazed and struggling to take things in. He then tends to Jem again.

Is Jem dead?

Then he's not dead?

Far from it. He's got a bump on the head just like yours, and a broken arm.

Now I may be wrong, of course, but I think he's very alive. Go have a look at him.

You all right, Scout?

Yes sir, I'm goin' in to see Jem. Atticus 'n' them's in there.

I'll go with you.

 • How do we know Scout's still in shock?

In Jem's bedroom, Heck Tate shows them some things he has found. Then he tells them what else he found under the tree.

He can't hear you, Scout, he's out like a light. He was coming around, but Dr Reynolds put him out again.

Come in, Heck. Did you find anything?

I found a little girl's dress.

Bob Ewell's lyin' on the ground under that tree ... with a kitchen knife stuck up under his ribs.

Somehow, I could think of nothing but Mr Bob Ewell saying he'd get Atticus if it took him the rest of his life. Mr Ewell almost got him, and it was the last thing he did.

- The strange countryman in the shadows – who is he?
- A coward to the end, why does Bob Ewell attack the children?
- Who was the other vulnerable person Bob Ewell tried to intimidate? See page 61.

Heck gets Scout to tell them what has happened. He examines her costume. There is a shiny, clean line on the chicken wire that formed the shell of her costume – clearly made by a knife.

This thing probably saved her life ... Bob Ewell meant business ... Low-down skunk with enough liquor in him to make him brave enough to kill children.

Scout continues.

Jem hollered.

There was this funny noise ... Mr Ewell was tryin' to squeeze me to death ... then somebody yanked Mr Ewell down.

Who was it?

Scout suddenly realises who has saved their lives.

Why, there he is, Mr Tate, he can tell you his name. Hey, Boo ...

• Boo Radley has not been able to face anybody for 15 years. Why did he come to the aid of the children?

• How do Boo's actions relate to what Atticus said about courage on page 36?

The murder weapon is a kitchen knife, still in the body. Heck uses a switchblade knife. He *says* he took it off a drunk earlier in the evening, to demonstrate how Bob Ewell fell.

I don't want my boy starting out with something like this over his head ... I don't want anybody saying, 'Jem Finch ... his daddy paid a mint to get him out of that.'

Bob Ewell fell on his knife. He killed himself.

It was like this.

Atticus thinks Jem might have grabbed the knife from Bob Ewell and must stand trial. Heck Tate is absolutely sure that Bob Ewell fell on his own knife, therefore letting Jem and Boo 'off the hook'.

See there? Stabbed himself ...His whole weight drove it in.

I won't have it.

God damn it, I'm not thinking of Jem!

It ain't your decision ... it's all mine. It's my decision and my responsibility ... There's not much you can do about it.

- Who is Heck Tate thinking of?
- Did Heck find the switchblade at the scene of the crime? Could that have been Bob Ewell's knife? If so, where did the kitchen knife come from?
- Who killed Bob Ewell?

Heck Tate doesn't want the public to know that Boo was present at all. He stands up for what he thinks is right, which means that there can be no trial.

- 'Let the dead bury the dead'. What do you think Heck Tate means?
- Why does Scout liken injuring Boo to killing a mockingbird?

- Look at page 15 again. Can you find another instance of common sense and kindness being more important than sticking rigidly to the law?

70

'Will you take me home?'

He almost whispered it, in the voice of a child afraid of the dark.

Boo and I walked up the steps to the porch. His fingers found the front door-knob. He gently released my hand, opened the door, went inside, and shut the door behind him. I never saw him again …

I looked behind me. To the left of the brown door was a long shuttered window. I walked to it, stood in front of it, and turned around. In daylight, I thought, you could see the post office.

Daylight … in my mind, the night faded. It was daytime and the neighbourhood was busy. Miss Stephanie Crawford crossed the street to tell the latest to Miss Rachel. Miss Maudie bent over her azaleas. It was summertime, and two children scampered down the sidewalk towards a man approaching in the distance. The man waved, and the children raced each other to him.

It was still summertime, and the children came closer. A boy trudged down the sidewalk dragging a fishing-pole behind him. A man stood waiting with his hands on his hips. Summertime, and his children played in the front yard with their friend, enacting a strange little drama of their own invention.

It was fall, and his children fought on the sidewalk in front of Mrs Dubose's. The boy helped his sister to her feet, and they made their way home. Fall, and his children trotted to and fro around the corner, the day's woes and triumphs on their faces. They stopped at an oak tree, delighted, puzzled, apprehensive.

Winter, and his children shivered at the front gate, silhouetted against a blazing house. Winter, and a man walked into the street, dropped his glasses, and shot a dog.

Summer, and he watched his children's heart break. Autumn again, and Boo's children needed him.

Atticus was right. One time he said you never really know a man until you stand in his shoes and walk around in them. Just standing on the Radley porch was enough.

- Over two and a half years, Scout and Jem have learned many things. Scout has learned to use her head, not her fists, and the nature of true courage. They have both learned about prejudice, racism and the need to protect the weak.

- Look back through the story. Remind yourself when and where they came across these new ideas.

Scout returns home, reflecting that there wasn't much left for herself and Jem to learn – except possibly algebra. Atticus reads her a story and tucks her up in bed. Sleepy and confused, mixing the story and reality, she mumbles to Atticus. As usual, he knows just what to say …

• Scout and Jem have learned a lot, and they will go on learning. When do you think they will stop?

• How many 'mockingbirds' can you find in the story?